In My Father's House

DAVID KINLOCH was born in Glasgow in 1959. His previous books of poetry include *Dustie-fute* (Vennel Press, 1992), *Paris-Forfar* (Polygon, 1994) and *Un Tour d'Ecosse* (Carcanet, 2001). Other publications include studies of the French writers Joseph Joubert and Stéphane Mallarmé, as well as work in the field of Translation Studies. For many years a teacher of French, David Kinloch now teaches creative writing and Scottish literature in the Department of English Studies at the University of Strathclyde.

T0294084

Also by David Kinloch from Carcanet

Un Tour d'Ecosse

DAVID KINLOCH

In My Father's House

CARCANET

First published in Great Britain in 2005 by
Carcanet Press Limited
Alliance House
Cross Street
Manchester M2 7AQ

'Tremmlin Tree' is a translation of 'Espenbaum'; 'Daithfugue' is a translation of
'Todesfuge', from Paul Celan, *Mohn und Gedächtnis* © 1952 Deutsche Verlags-Anstalt,
Stuttgart. 'Assisi' is a translation from Paul Celan, *Von Schwelle zu Schwelle* © 1955
Deutsche Verlags-Anstalt, Stuttgart. 'Ye caun traistly' is a translation of 'Du darfst mich
getrost'; 'A dunnerin: it is' is a translation of 'Ein Dröhnen es ist'; 'In waters nor o thi future'
is a translation of 'In den flüssen nördlich der Zukunft', from Paul Celan, *Atemwende*,
© Suhrkamp Verlag, Frankfurt am Main 1967. 'Because ye fund the trauchleskelf' is a
translation of 'Weil du den Notscherben fandst', from Paul Celan, *Fadensonnen* © Suhrkamp
Verlag, Frankfurt am Main 1968. 'Knock thi' is a translation of 'Klopf die' from Paul Celan,
Lichtzwang © Suhrkamp Verlag, Frankfurt am Main 1970. 'Tenebrae' is a translation from
Paul Celan, *Sprachgitter* © S. Fischer Verlag GmbH, Frankfurt am Main 1959. 'The skyrin'
is a translation of 'Die hellen Steine' from Paul Celan, *Die Niemandsrose*,
© S. Fischer Verlag GmbH, Frankfurt am Main 1963.

A CIP catalogue record for this book is available from the British Library
ISBN 1 85754 766 7

The publisher acknowledges financial assistance from Arts Council England

Typeset by XL Publishing Services, Tiverton
Printed and bound in England by SRP Ltd, Exeter

Contents

Acknowledgements

Thanks are due to the editors of the following magazines where some of these poems first appeared: *Chapman*, *PN Review*, *Painted*, *Spoken*, *The Paper*.

'Dancing in the Archives' was commissioned by the Scottish Screen Archive.

I should like to thank the Stifleson Foundation, Sweden, the Scottish Arts Council and the National Library of Scotland for a Robert Louis Stevenson Memorial Award which enabled a stay at the Hotel Chevillon, Grez-sur-Loing, France, where this collection was finished.

I should like to acknowledge John Felstiner's exceptional commentary *Paul Celan: Poet, Survivor, Jew* which provided much guidance and stimulation when working on the Scots translations of Celan's poems.

'The Earth Dies Too', 'Belonging' and 'Tae Rimbaud' are versions of poems by Mohammed al-As'ad, Walid Khaznadar and Mou'in Bsissou, based on translations in Abdellatif Laâbi, *La Poésie palestinienne contemporaine, choix des texts et traductions*, Le Temps des Cerises et la Maison de la Poésie Rhône-Alpes, 2002.

With gratitude, as ever, to Eric for his support and patience, and particular thanks to Richard Price for his eagle-eyed criticism as well as for his friendship while this book was being written.

In Memory of my Father

In My Father's House

I Set Off Upon my Journey to the House of Shaws

Well, Davy-lad, it is lychgate time:
Dad's coffin pausing between two worlds.

Look how the good frock-coated minister of Essendean
pours you tea beneath its wooden canopy.

The dead breakfast in the rafters
like windchimes in a nearby garden.

Soon a letter will bear a story of inheritance,
a round giftie, a square giftie and the niceties will fall away.

You'll fill your satchel, put a packed lunch in a tuck box
and set out for the Tower of Living Stone.

'The House of Shaws!' cried I,
'What had my poor father to do with the House of Shaws?'

Prospect the sediment of 'shaw':
it gives compacted 'foliage of esculent roots',

a tower of turnips and potatoes,
a living herbage hard as undernourished stone;

deeper still, the teutonic
'schawe', a wood, a grove:

see how simply the floors
collapse upon each other
from the impact of overloaded words:

And in a schaw, a litill thar besyde
Thai lugyt thaim, for it was nere the nycht

and wood gave 'shade' gave 'shadow',
gave all the 'schawaldouris',
the wanderers in woods
who fell with all their words
through floors of wood and stone,
dustie-futes all, taken in mid-life,
wandering among the roots
and tubers of tall towers.

Steady lad
canny goer
good pillow
blithe and soople
here's your shilling piece
the little pickle money
of tremulous and cholic
big rowans where my father lies

Loch Morar

My bright red Camper shoes
at Back of Keppoch's jetty
taste the golden mustard
pods of seaweed,
giving me treasure
of their cracked light.

And from my heels
the long sleek animal
of shore – its mat, its satin
blacks – flees back,
sucks gently on the sea.

'David!' Dad's voice
tries to stop me tempting
Eden, overlaying snap
upon snap: feathers
of mares' tails, the fraying shreds
of azure rope and streams
of birdsong, Chinese in its complexity.

'David! We're going now!'

But he drove us to Beauty
each year never fail.
Months ahead he'd hunter-
gather miles of motorway,
fleece 'ideal spots' of February
snows and imagine his family
there until they were:

always at the end of minor
cart-tracks; we lived
in passing places, my mother's
anxious face lop-sided from her
angle in the ditch; set down

among a scatter of cottages
and bungalows whose ragged
lace interiors seemed at home
in disarray, as if inside wasn't
thought of much amid the stray
and windy sunshines.

Bracora! Bracorina! Brinacory!
Litters of ruined shielings
just rubble by the Loch;
yet every plot
is like a miniature continent,
each with its hillock,
its rabbit-burrowed, hollow
sounding ground,
seal-headed eilans
slumming it in coves.

On his evening walk
Dad would gesture to it,
saying nothing, stretch his arms
wide, again and again,
as if he wanted to give it all
to us forever; suddenly

his body was a half-moon chasuble
snaked by trickling burns,
heather sprouting from his oxters,
embedded mica sparkling on his brow.
Here he elevated Nature
Host of holidays!

And at home he offered Art:
opera or amateur theatricals.
That summer by Loch Morar
he prepared to be Macbeth
on his return to Glasgow,
drove us superstitiously around
and my mother half-demented.

One night three thousand, three hundred
and thirty-three giant moths
battered through their room
as we ran screaming
from the bothy, Dad muttering
'Dunsinane! It's Dunsinane!'

And next day his children
buried him in sand and patted
hard until he couldn't move.
Still I see her: Lady Macbeth
on the Silver Sands of Morar
digging out her husband
with a frail toy spade.

Moths, motes of sand, monsters
thronged my competing fantasies:
Mhorag, Nessie's cousin
or leap-year alias
who swum a deep and submarine

passageway from Loch to Loch,
enthralled a monster Kingdom
beneath the mountains,
tutored schools of monsterlets
in monster lore: I could go on and did.

In a cave of dunes,
silent, intense and hot,
I waited for Mhorag to burrow
through to me, so we could burrow
back together, to the shadowless
Loch on the other side, waited
so we could jump

the life to come and swim,
discarding custom, costume,
monstrously naked in ruby
flesh: truly incarnadine.

But Dad said 'Monsters do not change
their spots.' How did he know?
Oh he did, just did, just did.

Avalon

Two photos, like apples dooked in Time,
rest on each palm.
Nicotine-skinned September snaps
– just on the turn –
they curl windfalls of flesh
into the pentacled core of your hands.

Hands shuffle, divining:
three crab-apple dolls
stuck on dowels
with yarn for hair.
The children sit cross-legged at a Druid's feet:
Dad as Orovesa from Bellini's *Norma*.

Up he towers towards a white
Egyptian-looking bunnet,
a golden sickle of papier-mâché
growing from his fist.
Oaken, belted in mistletoe,
his gaze exhorts groves of absent faces
with a Celtic coloratura.

The second photo shows Chuma and Susi,
also cross-legged, awkward in outsize suits,
posed before the altar of their Master's relics:
David Livingstone's cap. His maps and sextant.
The famous lion that wounded him in sketches,
skinned and roaring before a trunk
draped in Union Jacks.

It's like a dumb supper's table
set with places for the dead
and that trunk was once a tree.
Hollowed out to make a casket
for Livingstone's embalmed corpse,
they logged it, lugged it,
shipped it in a canvas flag for home.

Two photos: two empty trunks that fill
with the sap of wandering, climbing children.
'Where', they wonder,
'are his real sons and daughters?' Or,
'What is a Druid's family?' Just
trees, trees, trees?

They meander through the jungles
of that fathomless apple tree,
each belled branch an unmapped river
tinkling with pagan leaves.
Boughs creak amid the prayers
of little idol huts and from another twig
a minor Donizetti swings the baubles of good tunes.

Stuck in wait-a-bit thorns
the children press on lumps of rose-quartz
fast in red, pink-ribboned bags
that dangle in the breeze,
glance up the maypole glimmer
of the moonlit apple trunk
and find it tipped in Avalon.

Not the Nile's source
in the Fountains of Herodotus, no:
that's in a non-existent space
conjured by a dropped chronometer,
but our Fathers without their Druid robes,
perched like spiritual robins
drunk on toast we've dooked in cider,
our Fathers: real, alive and singing.

Clootie tree tied up
in our deepest wishes
O weather wish
away to true

Ralph

Once she had left the garden, Ralph,
you hung back and with that shipwrecked
penknife and Peterkin's
old–German silver pencil case,

you carved out that gigantic
sternum, that singer's chest,
from your own silk flanks,
gave Dad those instruments
of his creation as weapons
for his war against the White Witch
in battle for Prince Caspian.

Cardross was *Cair Paravel*,
euphonous above Clyde's estuary
and the far ships' fog horns
muscled in like the lion–god
Aslan through the night.

In return Dad made you
complete and unabridged,
High King, coral boy,
iridescent as the sewage strewn reefs
that skirted Helensburgh,
her fleets, her floss, her promenade
of bowling greens.

I Presume

In this opera my Dad is Doctor
Livingstone lost in inclement bush
and I am Stanley trying to think
what I will say to him across the rapids
of our handshake.

It is Act 3: a bank of krieg lights
blanch unstinted draughts of a water-hole
putrid with the stage-designer's
vision of rhinoceros dung.

I am in the pit of doubt
unwinding a recitative:
'Commit thy way unto the lord
and he shall direct thy steps.'
I stumble on the phrase:

'Is this all gammon?'
and on cue my head turns
back: 'Doctor Living
stone, I presume':
a statement of his presence.

He seems to die before me:
unaccompanied, he crumples
on the sedgy grass but then
the hell of music takes him
for the Don he is:

bramble papyrus thick as a wrist
wraps about his feet as he
arpeggios down like hippos
of the flooded valleys,
entering embezzled 'discoveries',

the humid theatre of his past
where he arranged 'beyond
every other man's line of things'
ritornellos of rivers,

navigable highways to arias
of liveable plateaux: fantasies
of a fake missionary
and missionary 'murderer!'

I presume your family craved an ending
to the hundred and seventy-six
verse psalms of greasepaint
rife with prodigious ticks and lice,
recognition that the tales of

falls were true. I presume
your son devoutly wished
God's song would stop:
it finally did

and in the darkness
emanating from the flies
we discover a silence
at the heart of music,
even in the silent stave.

I sleep upon one note of hope:
that brief strain –
was it prologue or flashbacked
epilogue? – those tears
when you dropped your oatcake
in the burn at Hamilton.

A Cardross Callas

For my caterwauling, my little
soldier-like refusal to eat
her plain poached eggs,
she 'wheesht!' me
one last time then lost it,
shut me in the attic to bewail my
slimecoveredmaggoteaten
disemboweleddeadinacarcrash
Mum and Dad who'd parked us
for the weekend with our Gran.

A whole cold night later
saw her supplicant at the keyhole
trying to calm my sniffs
though still *adamant on punishment*,
telling me the story of how she got her voice,
of how an angel knelt
at the eyelet of her ear
and filled its honeycomb
of pink canals with music
making her the 'Callas of Cardross'.

Quite flummoxed, I primly
asked her what she gave the angel
in return. There was a pause.
And then the keyhole sang
without a tremor,
her voice full in the grain
of the lock, unlocked
and clear: 'an apple',

'an apple from my garden'.
The angel, caught up
by some familiar air,
took the apple but let her keep
the apple's voice instead,
a sound that added
such value to her throat
it thronged with songs
that dropped from trees
and made the angel smile.

Even at the time
it struck me she was lucky –
not being great or good
or particularly holy –
to get an angel in her house.
But right away I hunkered down
and whispered through the keyhole
'Can I just have one too?'

Poached eggs, they put me in the attic.
Angelic apples got me out.

Pagliacci

Tonight, Svetlov thrusts
his bearded bass into Babi Yar:
'It seems that I am a boy in Bialystok,
that I am Dreyfus.'
And yet blood barely stains
sweetie munchers of the Concert Hall,
young couples, sweatered from the same ball of wool,
coughers coughing for the sake of it
and not from the ice cold
breath as it escapes
the chambers of his voice

escapes them as it must.

That night, Dad Pagliacci'd
our front room with his stentorian baritone,
frightened his small sons
back beneath a tent of sheets
behind the pink settee,
coaxed them out to hear their father
with a paunch of stockings
our mother knitted up for him.

And there on the savannah
before the piano stool,
we clapped the monstrous
hunchback of our Daddy,
knowing it was Daddy,

then blinked and ducked
within the tiny ghetto
of our encampment,
– opera within a minor opera –
plugged our ears
against the way his tears
went major,
flicked shut the flap
against the furnace of his voice
and took each other's hand
in our cool space.

Tonight, Svetlov takes
the flounce of Brussels lace
upon his face, the jab
of parasol, of boot and nail.
He sounds the soundless
scream that we must hear
within the comfort of our concert
tent whose mammoth walls
quaver with Mum's shadow
passing gently like the Magi
over the steppe of Babi Yar
and the weeping wildebeest
of my little brother
'I am Anne Frank'
'Nò! Pagliaccio non son!'

Tremmlin Tree

efiir thi German o Paul Celan

Tremmlin tree, your leaves blink white intae daurk
Ma mither's hair wiz nivver white.

Dainty-lion, so green is the Ukraine,
Ma lint-white mither didnae come hame.

Rain clud, dae ye swither at the well?
Ma lown mither greets for all.

Roondit stern ye rowe the gowden loop
Ma mither's hert wiz hurt by lead.

Aiken door, wha hoised ye aff yer hinges
Ma douce mither cannae come back.

Tremmlin tree – aspen; dainty-lion – dandelion; lint-white – white as flax, flaxen
blond; clud – cloud; swither – be uncertain, move fitfully; lown – quiet, subdued;
greet – weep; rowe – roll, coil; aiken – oaken; hoised – raised, hoisted; douce – gentle.

The Cure

for Eric

My bogeyman was a gorgeous blond
who stole my bike when I was ten.
I got the even bigger boys to beat
him up. So then he hatched a plot:
a chain of roughs from Daisy Street
sprung up around the tennis club
where I snuck down, peeped out
from mottled window panes
and listened to my fear trip
loudly on the wooden floors,
a butterfly in clogs.

Through time Mum sallied forth
in the Morris Oxford from our house
across the road. Still aproned
from a dinner she'd laboured
at for hours, she didn't need
a rolling pin. Just looked at them
and me. Since then I've been a hero.

'Ye caun traistly'

eftir thi German o Paul Celan

Ye caun traistly
ser me wi snaw:
whenever shouder tae shouder
ah stapit thru simmer wi the mulberry
its smaaest leaf
skreicht

Traistly – safely; ser – serve; skreicht – screeched.

Psychomachia

A is digitised ink, arrival's initial:
it speaks of inhabited stones, skiffing
mud in flat-bottomed boats,
of schist and marl and silt,
grain for Le Mont St Michel.

A boy with wings in old Aubert's dream
began this storied place,
with an A for abbey, tied to a rock,
pinned down with archivolt bands.

B is for boy, boy
who tolls in my mind
like that *cloche de brume*,
belling us, pilgrims through fog,
unsure of each other,
between brother and lover.

Here are the clichés that show us
in monks' *meditatio*
gabbling a guidebook aloud:
in this one, the sun has picked out
a tattoo on his biceps,

manuscript flesh that unscrolls
a miniature map of the Mount;
it swells and unfolds
emblazoned escarpments,
veined towers of blue and gold stone.

My fingers trace out mussel
shells – or sun-changed
lilies of France inked up
in a cloistered grey –
follow the liminal skein
of terrace and trelliswork,
touching up memory,
margins of skin.

We float on the film,
breathless *in-pace*
of monkish shapes
that cry for a vocative 'O!'
to hold back the fade-out,
to mouth out and focus the colour,

busy scriptorium bodies
initials criss-crossing like vine-leaves,
entwining the vault of an A,
equally lord, equally vassal,
allowed by a carnival quill.

But the word is quite lost
in the shuffle of photos:
your shoulder turned in
to the cold of the nave
is pumice smooth,
white as a parchment.

And there, in another, the figure
is tiny, a barely perceptible gesture,
staved between froth and water
by the edge of the washland erasure.

See how it flees from a snail
in this *bas-de-page* picture,
a one-legged sciapod,
sand dervish jousting the whelk slough,
lancing the mount of its body.

How all the *grisaille* surfaces
shimmer at prime or vespers
and St Michel levitates,
sainted and weightless,
framed high above me
out of reach of my barb and my gloss.

A is for *abbé*, for *abba*
– that's 'Daddy' in Hebrew,
Father of rose and clerestory –
a rhyme scheme to tie
this meandering grief
down to the point of its pain.

Song

Stopping to sniff
in the leidered flaw,
to note the motes
of aeolian plankton,

Tiggywinkle, mole-like,
lost in the marvel
of Ilm's infinite meadows,
Fichte falls from a raft

that ferries the flood,
shoos Schubert through ryegrass,
away from the locks of glissandos,
his tune on the tip of a key-change:

Weimar und Weimar
Weimar und Weimar

Thus the song or
thus the song just
levitates out of its glow,
laral and gardened,
designed of *Dasein*:

Weimar und Weimar
Weimar und Weimar

Hark to its culture of fish,
of oysters, of bees in silk,
the little narrative
of temperate tillage
on groundswells
of dowager labour;

song of good vicinage,
aimiable views of harvested fields,
the clefs of the mallow walk,
the staves of tanned bark,
the lyrical kiln
of drying prunes:

Weimar und Weimar
Weimar und Weimar

But then there's that quaver,
that tremulous tremolo,
a breeze on the pages of *Faust*
fast in the light poplar cabinet

and the three vows
'industry', 'veracity', 'consistency',
that sobbed in Heidegger's silence:

Weimar und Weimar
Weimar und Weimar
Weimar und Weimar

Daithfugue

eftir thi German o Paul Celan

Black milk o day-daw we drink it at een
we drink it at noon an the mornin we drink it at nicht
we drink an we drink
we shovel a grave i the lyft whaur ye'll no ligg tae tight
A maun bydes i the hous he flytes wi his snakes he scrieves
he scrieves when it's gloamin tae Deutschland yer gowden herr
    Margarete
he scrieves it an staps ower the door an the sterns are aw bleezin he wheeps
    his hunds ower
he wheeps his Jews oot lets thaim shovel a grave i the yird
he bids us flyte noo fur the daunce

Black milk o day-daw we drink ye at nicht
we drink ye the mornin at noon we drink ye at een
we drink an we drink
A maun bydes i the hous he flytes wi his snakes he scrieves
he scrieves when it's gloamin tae Deutschland yer gowden herr
    Margarete
Yer ashen herr Shulamith we shovel a grave i the lyft
    whaur ye'll no ligg tae tight

He yowls howk the yird deeper yous lot yous ithers sing an flyte
he grabs fur the cosh in his belt he swings it his een are sae blue
howk deeper yous lot wi yer spades yous ithers flyte mair fur the daunce

Black milk o day-daw we drink ye at nicht
we drink ye at noon an mornin we drink ye at een
we drink an we drink
a maun bydes i the hous yer gowden herr Margarete
yer ashen herr Shulamith he flytes wi his snakes

He yowls flyte mair douce-like wi daith this daith is a maister frae
    Deutschland
he yowls scrieve yer strings daurk-like ye'll stour lik smeik tae the lyft
ye'll then hae a grave i the cluds whaur ye'll no ligg sae tight

Black milk o day-daw we drink ye at nicht
we drink ye at noon Daith is a maister frae Deutschland
we drink ye at een in the mornin we drink an we drink
this Daith is a Maister aus Deutschland his ee it is blue
he drills ye wi bullets o leid drills ye richt weel an true
a maun bydes i the hous yer gowden herr Margarete
he sets his sleuth-hunds on us gies us a grave i the lyft
he flytes wi his snakes an drames Daith is a maister frae Deutschland

yer gowden herr Margarete
yer aschen herr Shulamith

Day-daw – daybreak; een – evening; lyft – air, sky; ligg – lie; byde – live, stay; flyte
– play, scold; scrieve – write; gloamin – dusk; gowden – golden; herr – hair; stern –
star; wheep – whistle; yird – earth, ground; hund – hound; howk – dig; yowl – shout,
scream; stour – rise up; smeik – smoke; leid – lead; drame – dream.

Thresholds

i.m. William Jeffrey (1896–1946), Margaret Jeffrey (1898–1990)

Two motes of something float
down in sunlight, seed floating sidie-
ways, (drawing your eyes to the lip,
the sill,
that filament of flesh edging
cornea and rim and lid),
a wisp of threshed corn.

The heat's ignition cuts
out: breath baited
in the 'tick tick tick'
of our summer train
marking time in Arrochar Station.

Definitions, roots of the word
'threshold' bud in our warm
carriage-bath
with its 'freshwood' doorway
to the corridor beyond.

'*The threshwort's worn
quite hollow down*'
and in the silence
and the birdsong soft-
pedalled through our window

we sense a solitary
Station Master (just out of
sight) tending to the Holy
Grail:

there is a libation of quietness;

then, a clunky slam
of a big steel lock
clasping the hasp
of a door: a hunky
cyclist – maybe – gets on.
We see no one, wait
for the whistle.

This moment is before
Scheherazade begins to read.
The astounded air
is rapt.

This moment David Livingstone,
lugging 'Pearl'
through African mud,
pauses in the after-
flash of a kingfisher's
dive.

No; fingering the warm
bevel of the window-frame,
you bracket the exotic
and float – again –
into your body's
border times, where it borders
on others, your pasts,
their pasts: the hesitations

of puberty: ravishing
silk gloss of the bra pages
in Brian Mills's catalogue
thumbed to a palimpsest
through which the Calvin Klein
Y's glow like white clouds of unknowing.

Those moments in Maths class
when the teacher, hugging
knees to chin, shuffles
the fates of Orpheus
and you swither from one
to the other, swither

as my poet grandad did
two trenches down from Owen
and Sassoon. Deep
in the same 'profound dull tunnel'
he couldn't quite catch
the rhyme of 'groaned'
with 'groined' which grazed
him as his tongue turned
back and petrified in myth.

Dumbfounded by belatedness,
eventually he wept with fear
for his small family,
and pushed his trembling,
Parkinson-bent body
back from the office
through the Clydebank
blitz and in his second
war now heard the true
pitch of the bombs' rich rhymes,
pushed through that threshold
and died among a handful of good poems.

A disembodied brush
on the station platform
sweeps memory into language:
we step into the space between
as into the pure, thin
air of Translation,

where they ask of a piece by Arvo Pärt
repeating on the Walkman

'What kind of music is this?
Whoever wrote it left himself
behind to dig piano notes
out of the earth.'

And you know these slightly out-of-
kilter gestures look beyond their source
to a more wonderful country
that is not really there.

No platform
in the land of Wordsworthian
epiphanies: they are not far,
may not exist at all, hover
on the brink of being.

This is a 'Gateway to the Highlands',
a sunlit body on the verge
of cumming where you cannot hold
back and do
before a silence absorbs you
so lasciviously
all the breathable air
is sucked out of the carriage.

It deposits you once more
before that night-time
doorway to hear the chasms
of loss sob within your grandma
on the brink of her extinction –
Tick   tick   tick –
your footstep, your spying
ear, mote of dandelion
in the lychgate's shade,
a wisp of long white hair
lifting in the little summer
breeze waiting for me
to step up to her beyond
the threshold of her room.

The Earth Dies Too

after the Arabic of Mohammed al-As'ad

Stars offer the trees
their confident shade

and echo speaks echo
as street quits street

for homes of shut doors
which whisper behind them:

Do our witnesses speak
of us, whisper us, echo us?

How can we possibly say?

How can we possibly
chatter away, as if others –

the papers, the TV, air
timetables – sipped at our coffee,

as if we were right there with them
as if they were right there with us?

The earth dies too
into empty roads
into lonely houses
and lost countrysides.

The earth dies too
in the fug of town lights
in the dead of nights
in Uni diplomas
fresh orange juices
and twilights, twilights.

Worry, worry in the soul
is not just in the soul

it's in that polished calm
that piles up on desks

on the worn settee,
on coffee spoons, cradles

that corner a bedroom.

Why are we suddenly left
season less
sky less
father less?

All fade and fall
from windows and leaves
our desultory chats.

All leave us
until we come back
to the doorways of galleries,

the closed doors of supermarkets
come back like pavements,
deserted, strewn: the shrivel of summer.

The earth dies too
and can't absorb us
martyrs or prophets,

we whose suppression
is traceless
no clue to our absence,

we who spread out
like an untranslatable tenderness,
we who emigrate
like the uncontrollable nights
above unexplored deserts.

Roger Casement's Beard

for Christopher Whyte

> *And what if excess of love*
> *Bewildered them till they died*
> Yeats

Not 'Mutton chops' or 'French fork' or 'hulihee'
but a regular short boxed beard
held up Sir Roger Casement's head,

head firm very beautiful near the Casino
much bueno Agostinho huge testiminhos

an Antrim Imperialist Jingo beard
yet you can imagine how his delicate
tapering fingers stroked it,

stroked it, eyed constantly and wanted
a Caboclo seized hard. Young stiff and thin

tentatively at first, teasing out
nuances for Consular reports
on trade in rubber that never brought

brought me off finely. Rode gloriously.
Splendid steed. Huge, told of many. 'Grand'.

'Enlightenment' as Livingstone had hoped.
And then in true Conradian horror
how he must have held it

held it; brown eyes in suppurating bodies
Indian gentle men; soft as silk and big and full

in the jungles of the Putumayo
and the Belgian Congo.
King Leopold's was longer

long and curved no bush to speak of
Good wine needs no bush

and immeasurably more treacherous,
a liana of white rubber that stretched
from Brussels choking trees and men of sap.

sap sucker and cupped brown hands
about my face offering thanking petting

It could not compete with Roddie's
limpid baritone beard
that strolled with him into forests

forests and forests; Leopold occasionally
and myself, the incorrigible Celt

and out again six months later.
How it snagged in the bush
and then on the depravities of Irish politics,

the white Indians of Connemara the Bora boy's
broad good-humoured face like a Dubliner

snagged when Señor Normand had an Indian's
legs forcibly distended then beat him
in the pulpy crotch

crotch splendid; kissed the gift of thigh bone
the ivory smile of giving blush even through dark

until he died. How it bristled at the sound
of the chicotte that corkscrewed skin
with raw hippopotamus hide.

hide! slim fevered bones of the dear people
charity of shade, the douce socialist Amazonians

Trimmed and kempt even in extremis
it spoke of well kept property,
the parks of Congo, Brazil, Ireland

that park when I hope almost at once
to come across a good <u>big</u> one

but Casement's beard stiffened
only in the bonds of masculine affection,
the gentle caress of unsevered hands

hands of policemen wanting and one lovely
schoolboy, back and forward several times

that Capitalists often cut and smoke
on kilns and then preserve
as warnings of the Judgement Day.

You cannot call this beard 'whiskers'
though intermittently you imagine
a tiny Livingstone hacking up

the undergrowth to the dark gash
of his mouth and then his chest,
white but deep, particularly developed

thighs, the thighs and calves
of an indefatigable walker and his penis
at least comparable in health

to the black members
he itemised in diaries
with such relish.

When they stretched his neck
like a phallus teased
to fatal paroxysm,

his beard allowed him dignity
even in that final plunge
and it lay neatly on his corpse,

dark, youthful, vigorous,
without a trace of grey.

Post-mortem they probed
his hole for further evidence
of treasonable activity

and found it moist and black
as the Foreign Office
of Great Britain and Ireland.

met Friend who entered at once
Police passing behind paling – but he laughed
and went deeper. $10

Tenebrae

eftir thi German o Paul Celan

Nar are we, Lord
nar an at haun.

Haunlt awready, Lord,
clautin intae ilk ither, as if
ilka body, ilk ane were
your body, Lord.

Pray, Lord
pray tae us,
we are nar.

Wund-agley we gaed there
gaed there tae bend
ower pit an howe.

Tae the water-stowp we gaed, Lord.

It was bluid, it was
whit ye shed, Lord.

It glentit.

It kest your eemage intae our een.
Een an moo staun sae apen an empie, Lord.
We have drunk, Lord.
The bluid an the eemage that was in the bluid, Lord.

Pray, Lord.
We are nar.

Haunlt – grasped; clautin – clutching; ilka – each other; agley – askew; howe – hollow,
hole; eemage – image; moo – mouth; empie – empty; nar – near.

La Tour de Ganne

for Bernadette Plissart

Light never leaves the Tour de Ganne:
sun or moon infused, its stones
are ruined by their blanching.
Blanche de Castille and Jean le Bon,
Louis le Gros, Philippe le Bel,
the lovely names, the leading lights
who sired this tower in casual tyranny,
first touched the candlewicks in windows
and made the sandstone beacon-like
to harrows and dry clods.

Light still turned upon the Tour de Ganne
when painters of the light first lit
on Grez-sur-Loing with RLS in tow.
Fresh from the Land of Counterpane
you gazed from Chevillon's hotel
at peasant fathers bent for furrows
disappearing through the slight *sfumato*
that wreathed the village bridge in mist.
Reflections from sheets flyped
by washerwomen beneath their canopied 'lavoirs'
caught your glance which flickered
up the tower of lichen greys,
rustling with the river's glitter,

and lights played round the Tour de Ganne.
They beamed back down and warmed the one
stone step that grounded Chevillon's tight
wooden stair. And as you stepped with her,
talking small, just met and not yet loved,
upon its uneven mottled dip then suddenly,
all shuddered, tipped like a gangway as the stone
turned in its wake, a small white ship
caught in the Old High Lights your fathers
wrecked their lives on, revolving round the earth

to South Sea Islands and light the Tour de Ganne
could never hold a candle to. Yet Skerryvore,
Muckle Flugga, Fidra, Stroma, Dhu Heartach
were nothing compared to her, so unsuitable,
so much older, from so far away, a transgression
by Dad's lights, hard for him to bear and so you pressed
harder on the stone step's deep lit-up hardness,
a threshold 'somewhere between whispered speech

and singing': *pierres perdues* in sunlight on the Tour de Ganne.

Pictures at an Exhibition

Look at these English pictures – the very dew is on the ground.
                                        Critic at Paris Salon, 1824

The lord of the harvest
winnows the day,
scything in red sash
glints of the Stour,
its locks, its barges,
towpaths and meadows:
all of old England
fording the parquet
of Salon in Paris with us.

Mireille, my tongue never
tripped as it should
on those difficult syllables
as the wind does gently
in its perfect accent
over these Constable trees.

Your arm never wavered
nor rested on mine
before this late 'vernissage',
those clouds of poison
slow in your veins
imperceptible cirrus
when you taught me good French,
a grammar as true
as his yellow and white
putting sunlight on dew.

Mireille – *mon enfant, ma sœur* –
haymakers are distant
no taller than bere,
these fields that gust
with the vole's night-taken
scream are calm now
and held by the trees' swathe
showered in light.

The *Telegraph* waits for us
moored at Mistley,
each step that we take
is a port at our feet:
steadily then, inspect
cuffs of jackets
that hand us up
to the empty haywain.

Closer yet, gilded
and sundered on Golding's
front lawn, that light
under leaf – is it Constable's snow? –
like a palm cupping water
scooped to quench thirst,
there – catch light
on the brink of being light
in the pool of the tree!

For this we are here,
becoming the stone
of East Bergholt mills,
where the palette knife
thickens *this* life,
there, where we'll go

jinking behind
the laden haywain
to *our* century's France:
a boat-shaped house
and a wake of steps,
a garden lunch,
a boy loved in sun
by a boy of nineteen.

An image as posed as a photo
hid in the stack;
prize up the straw strokes,
you touch patches of skin,
filmy, pellucid,
and a *punctum*,
a *punctum* beats out
like a tiny gold heart.

Closer and closer and
the canvas suggests all is illusion:
love unrequited,
Dad dying at home,
while the son forced his idyll
to shape up as he dreamt it;
John Constable's wife
dead of TB and
behind the haywain
a cinema of passions
that move so fast
we mourn them in passing.

Now the other boy's father
dies in dementia
and Mireille clicks my photo
on gallery steps,
slips out a slice
of instamatic past,
says in slow motion:
'Look' and 'here' and 'boy'.

But my eyes are full
of that last dark canvas:
a deer at bay in a forest glade
and I hear the word 'see'
lost among bodies and skies.

An Encounter

In Cardross Cemetery:
'Iain Crichton Smith',

a poet so alive to death
it made him real at last.

Four rows down –
my father – Dad.

In this little theatre
of words I make for them,

my Dad, who sold his kingdom
for booze and metaphor,

keeping death's whinny
far down the neighbour's field,

steps out of character and passes
swiftly through the audience of midnight stones,

fleeing from this real dead poet
as if he'd seen a ghost.

Dancing in the Archives

for Keith Alexander

Just a man dancing crazily in front of a box; and this wooden box standing on a cart in the middle of the desert with the dunes arching behind like the mouth of an oven. A hundred in the shade and still he danced. But there was something about the way he moved that made us stare and keep staring. For this was dance and no dance at all: a kind of work shaking beauty from work, seeking its shape and measure in the simple limits of the cart and box.

A neighbour said: 'Dance being born!', another: 'He canny dance tae save himsel!'

I see feet beat-juggling through no-man's land, working for the moment they can rest and stop. A hell of heat and sweat. Dust devils spur him on but his gyrating body finds no final form to clothe it: ghosts of rigadoon and sarabande play about his feet, wisps of passepied, dune-surf, air-surf, palimpsests of romp and pas-de-bas.

The crowd begins to grow. All manner of instruments – fir wood, harps, psalteries and timbrels – begin to sound around this theatre of dancing fire. And the dance seems now like a sacrifice of jiving limbs and shouts of 'Yahweh!' 'Yahweh!' So then King David arches his arm towards the golden box and a covenant of light filled with motes of sand and cries beams back playing true notes upon his face, reeling movement through his body, instructing it how to step and stop in time.

Now Yahweh dances. Here is the little salsa of the flame's law, that tongue's hip-hop, his body a tipping gangway to a deeper dance: a place where we forget all roots and root in the dance itself, where the grin in the quick of an in-step, a dowsed jump, the precipice in your tummy, surge up like a lift and flower in smile. Here is the dance of a lord, the laws of a lord archived in bodies of movement flung out in frames of light. This is the thou shalt dance, the thou shalt shalt not dance: no dance without work, no work without dance, the savour of both tasted only in each other's face.

When it stopped there were two men there. But when you looked at them closely although one was young and one was old you could see they were the same man, a king dancing out of a king.

'A dunnerin: it is'

eftir thi German o Paul Celan

A dunnerin: it is
Truith itsel
stapit amang fowk,
i the mids o the
metaphorgowst

Dunnerin – rumbling; gowst – squall.

Ghost Seed

for Colm Tóibín

All jars: the train expires
as gyres of warm air
lollop the platform
like desert tumbleweed.

A smattering of dust
upon upholstery puffs
up and enters a cone
of summer light staved
between three floating
dandelion seeds:

a woman's face
wishes through shadows
of the coach.

Her spirit dusts me
with pollen of pain;
a gauze of needles
settles and through the mesh
of sweat and mustiness

the strong ghost of Mrs Yeats
transpires escorting
her old man across the shires
to younger loves,
returning alone to Ballylee.

All floats in the coach's
fetid bath of heat:
she blows the snub-headed, impotent seed
away, watches the wisps
thrash their invisible words.

Deep within my eyes
her memories coalesce
and she takes my body
for its pains: I deliquesce,

barely perceptible, browsing
Blake and Yeats, knowing
there is life beyond the death of sex
before the final change.

'In waters nor o thi future'

eftir thi German o Paul Celan

In waters nor o thi future
ah wap thi net oot, that you
swidderin wecht
wi stanescrieved
sheddas

Wap – cast; swidderin – hesitatingly; wecht – weight; sheddas – shadows; stane-scrieved – stonewritten.

Painting by Numbers

1   He knew only the briefest details and at times experienced the memory of this man simply as a pure incarnation of tenderness, the tenderness of a shadow that had momentarily stretched out a hand to touch him and then withdrawn before becoming fully human. So this man was a sill, a threshold that spread through his mind beyond its own indistinct boundaries in soft pastel gradations, half figurative, half abstract. In the house in which he was staying, only the bottom step of the staircase which spiralled up in wood and iron was made of stone, a creamy, pock-marked slab, ancient but also somehow fresh, a remnant and a promise. It was a step between two worlds and each time he pressed on it with his foot he made a wish, as if he were on the stile in the field above Dunkeld swinging between adolescence and adulthood.

2   At the centre of the back of the eye is an area about a millimetre in diameter known as the fovea. It is supposed to contain only cones. Light falling on this small area gives the sharpest colour definition. So when he looked closely at his face in the mirror and saw the black rod of himself staring back from his pupils he knew that behind or nestling within these tiny Russian dolls lay others. Those of a man irradiated by colour, stretched out languorously on cones of the fovea that thrust up like the trees of Fontainebleau Forest into the heart of his eyes giving them that iris blue he now had to turn into paint.

3   One day he came across an old dictionary of the Scots language. He flicked desultorily through it and gradually he found his lips moving as they attempted to sound out these strange, vaguely familiar words. What he liked about them was the way many of them through disuse had almost but not entirely shaken loose from their referents. They weren't purely aural textures, nor were they distressingly full of actual meaning. So he felt he might try to inhabit them for a while, allow them to associate with the objects, places, people in his life. He might even assign them new meanings and then watch or listen and maybe even paint as their old ones, as their etymologies tried to re-impose their meanings. These words might flyte with the paintings they produced or embed themselves in their textures, disappear almost entirely into the paint itself. He wanted neither abstraction nor representation but a fluid, tactile *métissage*. He wanted to paint sound dissolving into meaning and meaning frittering away into the joy of not having to mean anything at all.

4   When he looked at something or someone that moved him, he didn't
     paint what he saw – at least not to begin with – but the shock it induced
     in him. And this was a pattern of experience these Scots words seemed
     to confirm. It was not the little wall of definitions that seduced him
     initially but the colours and sounds they touched off within him. It was
     as if they weren't words at all but textures, aural, verbal textures to be
     savoured in the mouth and held in the ear. Obsolete or on the verge of
     obsolescence they nevertheless carried their past uses and misuses about
     them like torn veils, floating upwards from Lethe offering you the fading
     shapes of human concerns. And yet in that moment of apparently irre-
     sponsible volatility – these Orphic words that bounced in Rabelais, that
     thawed and fell as rain – they reminded the living language of its causes,
     its pain, its travail. The words still at work look up from their tasks and
     smile with a smile René Char tenderly calls 'cassé bleu'. From that sky
     blue fissure, regret hovers in the air for words unable to mean in a present
     fizzing with meanings yet there is also gentle gratitude for the mirror
     they hold up, a mirror in which the living words are reflected but in
     which they also glimpse shadows of all the other words they abut yet
     cannot be themselves, of the otherness of being they reach towards yet
     always fail to grasp and of their own ultimate obsolescence.

     And in these words which now whirled around him like musical chairs,
     each one inviting him to leap and sit, he also found the tantalising shape
     of the man he liked. He would paint a word chosen at random from the
     dictionary and then find him in the word before he in turn dissolved into
     the loveliness of lac or terre verte, pigment which formed shapes human
     and inhuman poised in the lychgate space of paint.

5   A cloak of canals hangs
     down the canvas
     on an autumn wash
     and tiny barges
     sail slug-like
     up to heaven.
     But who is the easel
     holding it all
     the wrong way up?

6   Always let the light, the fragments of Fontainebleau sky which seem so
     foreign to 'malagrugrous' shine through it. A word forged in despair yet
     there must have been a joy, a momentary uplifting of spirit in recog-

nising its lamp blacks, its ochres, the bruised space it is host to. For a word like this there was never any Altamira moment, even if 'malagrugrous' growls in your ear like the thunder of approaching bison. Only slow accretion of sound on tiny sound, shellfish sound ground from the corals of language which our tongues lick at, awash in seas of sound and meaning.

7   Nicholas de Staël writes 'Pictural space is a wall but all the world's birds fly there freely.' He propped the old Scots dictionary on the easel before him and stared at the little walls of definition, the pendant etymologies. What bird of a feather seeded them? An unknown, invisible bird. Or a Dodo, perhaps. As extinct as the words it flies among. It hops among the cliff tops, the declivities. So the painting took shape: great wings of paint perching on savant abbreviations, sensing sister senses on the up currant from gesso, brown verdaccio of the earth. It plummets. He remembered how a painter had invented a bird that never stops flying and gives birth in the air. He painted its birth cry wondering how a definition can bear to end, like music. And how it can bear not to. What entices the derivation, the deviation? A colour? A tenderness, unexpected, unwanted, the cry of desire this man had ripped from his throat? Who first deepened the meaning unconsciously, setting it off on its slow burn towards the weir? What was her name? Why her? Why then? He would like to know. Be able to tap the canvas, tap the dictionary, tap the side of his nose knowingly and say nothing.

8   In the past, sometimes he had carried a specific word around with him in his head. Like a pebble taken from a beach as a memento. He would carry it around sounding it out in his mind but never or rarely actually say it. But it would be there, subtly colouring everything he said and thought. Now and again he would be on the verge of pronouncing it. He'd spy an occasion where he thought it might be *à propos*. But because of that, precisely for that reason, he didn't say it. Pudeur? Avarice? And in his more grandiose moments he imagined it might settle one day in a sentence like that perfect phrase from Vinteuil's sonata or the little stretch of yellow brick in Vermeer's *View of Delft* celebrated in Proust's big book. Then the satisfaction it would give him could come as much from the knowledge that only he would be able to recognise its true value, its perfect music.

So he wondered when a word of this kind might jump out at him from his dictionary. And then one day he realised that of course he had it all along and that it was the name of the man that haunted him. Not a dead word in an old dictionary but the living name of a living human being.

9   The canvas is always already primed. All seems a brilliant gesso but it holds every colour as in a diamond box locked against weak eyes. Wink, open it, and your father's name, his dedication even, will appear in faint blue streams as from invisible ink upon the flyleaf of a Bible. You are the painter but the pentimenti of his mark glimmers through the canvas gilt with faint gold leaf. Tilt it to catch the sunlight. Tilt it away so you may make your own inscription, create your own shapes from the lamp blacks of an imaginary white. You feel like Pliny's Corinth girl, the first to trace charcoal round a beloved shadow on a wall or a man stepping from forest, the world's first journalist, scribbling down the silhouette of a figure with a god's head running away across the empty plain before you. It stretches as far as the frame.

Here are the beloved preliminaries which are codas too: you prep tints for faces and draperies, take a minever brush tempered with oil to make the pile on velvet, rub the surface with pumice to give the canvas teeth for binding, swither: cadmium mid, cadmium pale, pick lemon chrome for the thin glazings and scumblings and spend an age preparing smalt blue from finely powdered cobalt glass found only in the skies of Teniers. You lay the palette of words aside. All words are aside: to let the man speak from the canvas, invent a name for himself, although it is already given. It does not sound portentous although it fills the entire canvas. It is sweet with the modesty of mustardseed and birds in herb branches and straightaway it unloosens the latchet of your shoes. And in this modesty of parable you imagine he might escape all words. That this man of canvas, of heart-wood and sap-wood, buttery and crisp beneath the brush, could be new and for you alone. Still, unmoving, yet exuding and absorbing moisture from the air; his oils, resins and tempera forcing him to crack, spill out his treasure made of rest and motion.

Yet what looks back always – with the chalky, troubled look of fresco – is your father's eyes, his inscribed words thundering quietly on the painting's blank expanse. You begin the work: place a crumb of violet, last colour in the rainbow, ending the known, igniting the unknown, in a corner; or a smudge of Phoenician purple from Byblos, made from the pierced vein of a murex shellfish, the same colour that stained ten curtains of fine twined linen for the Covenant's Ark.

4 Shifts

after paintings by Alison Watt after portraits by Ingres

1 Metaphysical Tango

Tango my sheets
tiny fold: out reach
their shy tangent
before a swivel
tugs them in.

Trip up an evanescent
half-smile as it catches
my absent presence
– present absence –
out, nicked by the swag's
vast pleats.

I is not there is it
an other elsewhere

2 Erotic Duck

Ruck-up, side-step, purse and
pucker before she trails...
magniloquently.
Oh night-gown!
what a wash
on the raw cotton duck!

3 Dangerous pockets

If you stare for long enough
at dangerous pockets
a stamen will stick out
and tongue you with its fine, hairy stipple
in the most intimate of

60

In there you can just
hear the clickety click click
of a miniature sewing bee
– by Uccello perhaps –
where the knights have downed
their lances and stitch up
the folds of blue and rose *mazzochi*
to keep their faces shady.

4 *Zwiefalt*

Here is the lip and the sag
the deliberate drape of
zwichen-fall
becoming *Zwiefalt*
the surface deep
deepening to surface
once again. Oh shift
me into this *Fuscum
subnigrum*!

I want to be
down there in there
enveloped by these
white flaps which tip
slips into me.

Tango away bright Moitessier!
blind me cool Rivière
to the sarky work
of this suspended shift.

'Zwiefalt' is a term used by Heidegger to refer to the folded nature of being. It is
discussed briefly by Gilles Deleuze in his book, *Le Pli*, about Leibniz and the
Baroque. Moitessier, Rivière, Tournon were aristocratic ladies painted by Ingres.

'The skyrin'

eftir thi German o Paul Celan

The skyrin
stanes reenge thru the lyft, the skire-
white, the licht-
bringers.

They are for
no gangindoon, no sklytin,
no, skliffin. They gang
up,
like the flindrikin
mey-spink they spirl apen,
they soum
towarts you, ma lown yin,
you, ma leal yin – :

Ah see you, you pouk thaim wi ma
new, ma
Ilkamaunshauns, you pit thaim
inate the Skyre-Yince-Mair, whilk nane
need greet for nor nem.

Skyrin – bright, glittering; reenge – bustle about noisily; skire – bright; sklyte – fall
with a thud; skliff – shuffle; flindrikin – insubstantial; mey-spink – common wild
primrose; spirl – split ; soum – swim; float; lown – gentle; pouk – pluck; ilka – each
one; whilk – which; nane – none, no one; nem – name.

Remission

for Gerry McGrath

The rash of russet earth.
Strewn. For remission.

In the autumn
remission came for him,

folded back the cancer
and he seized the winter

space it left him, filled
it with his fruits, his songs

and in the glacial energy
of love borrowed from death

we were born. Then, he seemed
the place in which the immaculate

distant pines met their reflection:
the sure clasp of earth itself,

a steady ground that could not end.
After a fairy tale that took him

twenty years to tell, the Grez
birches shivered out their silver

and spring and summer came back
with his delayed remittance.

Lazarus

eftir thi Latin o Prudentius

for Andrew Philip

Lazarus, tell us o the rackle-haundit
voice o Christ at rapped the lairstane
whaur ye ligg slumpt in pit-mirk
lik a craw in mist. Tell us o the lip
o Charybdis, the kyle at curls around
the Earl o Hell's big hoose,
yon unkent burn aye trinlin fire.
At the lair's threshwart,
– haipit wi muckle stanes –
stauns the Lord an ca's his frien's name:
'Lazarus, come furth!'
Staughtway the stanes rowe back
an the ugsome grave ootpits
a livin corp, a diedman straughlin.
Oh, guid-sisters, lowse the linens lichtsomely!
Only the scent o strinkled spice is in the lyft:
camovine an corrydander, clow an nitmug.
Nae guff o bodily decay pirls up.
The een, aince weezin wi atter, blink,
sheen an skime lik keekin gless,
chowks are lit wi cramasie
at aince were pock yarred,
skin harlin aff an quick wi hotterel.
Noo the smashin man staps furth,
the slot o his briest lik a burn i munelicht.
Wha hae slaiked the thrapple o yon decrippit corp?
Only the man at gied him body,
wha sowfft thru the bree an glaur He mooldit,
wha smit the slumpy yird wi life.
O Daith, douce an doon-hadden noo,
Daith, aince stanedeif, sing smaa
an hearken tae the laa.

Wha hauds sic pooer? Confess:
Oor Faither alane protecks me frae yer hauns
an He is Jesus.

Rackle-handed – having powerful hands; lairstane – tombstone; ligg – lie; pit-mirk – intense darkness; kyle – a strait, a sound; unkent – unknown; trinlin – wheel, trundle; threshwart – threshold; haipit – heaped; muckle – big; rowe – roll; ugsome – frightful, horrible; straughlin – struggling; lowse – loosen, set free; lichtsomely – joyously; strinkled – sprinkled; lyft – air, sky; camovine – camomile; corrydander – coriander; clow – clove; nitmug – nutmeg; guff – stink; pirl – spiral; weezin – oozing; atter – poison, purulent matter; sheen – shine; skime – gleam with reflected light; keekin gless – mirror; chowk – cheek; cramasie – crimson; aince – once; yarred – marked; harl – peel; hotterel – festering sores; smashing – vigorous, strapping; slot – the hollow depression running down the middle of the chest; slaik – quench; thrapple – throat; sowfft – blow, whistle softly; bree – liquid, broth; glaur – mud, term of contempt for a person or thing; mooldit – moulded; slumpy – marshy, muddy; doon-hadden – kept in subjection; sing smaa – adopt a deferential or submissive tone; laa – law; pooer – power.

Assisi

eftir thi German o Paul Celan

Umbrian nicht.
Umbrian nicht wi the siller o bell an olive leaf.
Umbrian nicht wi the stane ye harlt here.
Umbrian nicht wi the stane.

Stumm, whit sprauchlt intae life, stumm.
Stech the stowp.

Stowp.
Stowp whaur the stowpmakkar's haun fessent.
Stowp that a shedda's haun shut fur ivver.
Stowp wi the shedda's seal.

Stane, whaur ye're glowerin, stane.
Lat the grimbeast in.

Trotshauchlin beast.
Trotshaughlin beast i snaw strewn by the naikitest haun.
Trotshaughlin beast afore the wurd clasht shut.
Trotshaughlin beast that gowps sleep frae yer haun.

Glent, that brings nae easement, glent.
The deid – they still gae cadgin, Franz.

Nicht – night; siller – silver; stane – stone; harl – haul; stumm – dumb; sprauchle – struggle, clamber; stech – stuff; stowp – jug; shedda – shadow; haun – hand; fessent – fastened; grim – grey; trot – jog, skip; shaughle – shuffle, walk clumsily; gowp – gobble; glent – glint, brightness; easement – comfort; cadge – beg.

Belonging

after the Arabic of Walid Khaznadar

Who has been in my room in my absence?
The vase of flowers is just off-centre.
The dead fighter's photo is no longer straight.
My papers seem to be composing themselves
    after a rapid scan.
That's not how I leave my shirt nor my pillow.

Who has been in my room in my absence?
What's happened here?
What kind of calm could nudge the vase back one inch?
How reconcile the dead fighter's look, the way he holds himself,
    to the wall's empty space.
Who will give back to my pillow, my shirt, the smell of a citizen?

'Because ye fund the trauchleskelf'

eftir thi German o Paul Celan

Because ye fund the trauchleskelf
on fell an muir,
the sheddacenturies sing dumb aside ye
an hear ye think:

Mebbe it's true
that twa fowks were forspoken here
oot o cley kists.

Trauchle – trouble; skelf – splinter; fell – steep hill; muir – moor; shedda – shadow; forspoken – conjured, brought forth; kist – vessel, pot.

Inquisition

The interviewer asks me about
'your homosexuality'
as if it were a mildly embarrassing
essential adjunct I carry
like a colostomy bag.

The interviewer asks me
'what your father would have
thought of it had he lived?'
when I know he knew,

dodged it every time he looked at me
because I was a mirror
and mourn him every day
because he died before he ever got to know me.

Impressions of Africa

And I am right
And you are right
And all is right as right can be!

The Mikado, Gilbert and Sullivan

Around four o'clock in the afternoon of June 25th, a red silk dragon trimmed with gold and studded with emerald sequins writhes in the tower of water like a sea horse. Air bubbles froth from its nostrils as the fabric slaps and sighs against a rock then drags along the shingle of the shallow ocean bed. Tiny minnows joust at its flame-like tongue but then dart swiftly away as a black hand grasps the dragon's head and pulls it upwards into sunlight. Similar actions are repeated all along the shore line as the strong young men of King Talou's tribe stoop in amazement to pluck purple cummerbunds and the odd lady, flummoxed in sodden petticoats, from the water. My father, clinging to the painted roof of a pagoda, stoutly refuses the proffered hands and swims manfully to the water's edge. There he is immediately arrested, his wrists tied behind his back and the entire troop of exhausted survivors marched through the forest to King Talou's village. In the distance the wreck of the *Lynceus* is etched like a pirate ship against the horizon. Were any of the party to turn in their manacles and look back they might hear music in the air.

*

Their path lies through a river covered with tikatika, a living vegetable bridge made by a species of glossy leafed grass, which felts itself into a mat capable, but only just, of bearing a man's weight. Its particularity is to bend in a foot or fifteen inches every step. This has the result – to the apparent hilarity of the Maruba fish which utters a cry and has breasts of milk – that some of the ladies nearly lose their footing and fall into the river. The muscular arms of the young Taloulians bear them up, however. In my father's case, it has the unfortunate effect of inducing motions not unlike those of sea-sickness. He falls to his knees and crawls to the end of the bridge. Much native laughter can be heard.

At length, having passed several huge traps for elephants, they come to the outskirts of the village, which is surrounded by fine gardens of bananas, groundnuts and cassava. These run up to a hedge some eighteen feet high and later inspection reveals that this is constructed of a kind of maize that bends its fruit-stalk round into a hook. The edifice is made by inserting poles that sprout like Robinson Crusoe's hedge, and never decay. Lines of climbing plants are tied so as to go along from pole to pole and the maize cobs are suspended to these by their own hooked fruit-stalk. This upright granary forms a solid-looking wall around the village. A little gate, concealed by a great mass of a species of calabash, is practised in its side and the party shuffles through, clanking past the crowd of women and children who throng around them in curiosity and derision.

*

King Talou is the tallest man my father has ever met. At a later stage in their relationship His Majesty will allow my father to take his measurements and record that the King stands just a little off seven feet in height. In all other respects, he is of firm and goodly proportions, his most remarkable feature being a head-dress woven of his own hair that reaches entirely around his head joining hair and beard together to create the effect of a halo. At regular intervals, large, wooden pins separate out the strands that resemble delicate, woven hirsute fans.

My father immediately prostrates himself before the King and gestures to his party to do likewise. He then identifies himself as Henry Morton Stanley, the Great Victorian Explorer. If only His Majesty understood English he might question the epithet 'Great' since Stanley's incompetent shipwreck has contrived to interrupt a game of chess he has been playing with his guest and old friend the Portuguese trader, whose name is not recorded in British annals of nineteenth-century exploration.

A patient man, however, he listens courteously as Stanley recounts his penurious upbringing in a Welsh workhouse, his flight to New Orleans aboard an American ship, his adoption by a prosperous wholesale merchant, his service in the Confederate Army during the American Civil War, his imprisonment in shockingly insanitary conditions, his debut as a journalist and finally his commission from James Gordon Bennett of the *New York Herald* to 'Find Livingstone!' The only word of this recitation King Talou understands is the word 'Livingstone'. He had met David Livingstone several years ago. Indeed, Dr Livingstone had interrupted an earlier game of chess with the same Portuguese trader and while he patiently answered the man's questions about local rivers found him something of a nuisance and a bore. Nevertheless, in return for a perfectly ugly string of beads – one has to accept something – he provided the said Doctor with a number of men and donkeys. The Doctor had departed seemingly content. In the intervening period, however, passing Arab traders impressed on King Talou the importance of not offering Livingstone any further help should he reappear. Apparently the man was every bit the nuisance King Talou had taken him to be. It is with these thoughts in mind that he now contemplates the still prostrate figure of Mr Stanley. Could Stanley be about to become a similar problem? The King strokes the five points of his luxurious beard and then settles his gaze upon the other members of Stanley's party.

At least Livingstone had brought no women with him but this man, this Stanley, has arrived accompanied by four women and four other men. He gets up and walks among the cowering prisoners. Something about the women's dress does not seem quite right. He has met Portuguese and British women before on a visit to Zanzibar prior to his accession to the throne. But the clothes these women are wearing, dishevelled and torn as they are, resemble nothing he has ever seen. He bends down and traces with his finger the shape of a red dragon on a silk sleeve. This is a strange animal, a veritable monster indeed. He grasps the frightened woman by the arm and hauls her to her feet. Stanley at once gets up and starts to explain: 'These are mere costumes Your Majesty. Not her real clothes. We were engaged in a rehearsal of a new operetta by Mr Gilbert and Mr Sullivan when the *Lynceus* hit rocks and foundered. We had no time to change, you see. The ladies in particular had been trying to get themselves into the spirit of their parts by wearing their costumes. They're Japanese. We were performing Mr Sullivan's latest piece *The Mikado*. Such diversions are necessary on long sea voyages.'

*

Perhaps you suppose this throng of epauletted fruit bats can't keep it up all day long. You're wrong you're wrong you're wrong, oh!

*

The Portuguese traveller, distracted from his near check-mate of King Talou by the commotion of the visitors' arrival, turns out to be an excellent linguist. The thespian enthusiasms of Mr Stanley's party once understood, King Talou – himself no stranger to the diversionary pleasures of spectacle – realises that the best way to prevent Mr Stanley from meeting Dr Livingstone and thus potentially doubling their nuisance value, would be to command a performance of Mr Sullivan's opera. Thus it is that Henry Morton Stanley and his troop of amateur players give the first performances on the African continent of that perennial favourite *The Mikado* en route to the 'discovery' of David Livingstone.

*

Initially dismayed by this needless interruption of his mission, Stanley concludes swiftly – after being presented with a human finger wrapped in a leaf – that his party has little choice in the matter. He now turns his attention to the means by which – with his superior European skills – he might gain the upper hand in this show of strength and eventually persuade the King to free them. As a pioneering ethnologist of distinction it does not take him long to decipher the cultural and religious co-ordinates of his hosts. Moreover, he is rapidly seduced by the charming affability of the young Taloulians who seem remarkably quick on the uptake, turn out to be natural actors and who count among their number several boys with quite wonderful voices. Stanley finds himself strangely drawn to one in particular, a certain Kalulu, whose lithe frame testifies to a range of manly virtues but whose voice has not yet broken. It is in the process of these discoveries that Stanley conceives his plot: *The Mikado* must be a joint production staged by visitors and hosts alike and there is nothing for it but that Kalulu must take the part of the virginal heroine, Yum-Yum, one of Mr Gilbert's enchanting 'three little maids from school', enamoured of the wandering minstrel Nankee Pooh. Stanley, who possesses a fine tenor voice, will inevitably take on the latter role while King Talou, he feels, will make an excellent Mikado. The rest of his party, entirely bereft in such circumstances of Stanley's sang-froid, acquiesce in his plans with little demur. Only Miss Conrad, deprived of her usual status as Yum-Yum, points out that King Talou in the title role of *The Mikado* which features multiple references to summary execution might be in the way of tempting fate. Stanley dismisses this observation as sour grapes.

*

Here are the mighty troops of Titipu: the turacos and fig addicted bulbuls, the bracts and ovipositors, geckos and cocktail ants and all the sweet sap exuded from the pores at the tips of Katisha.

*

It is not long before Stanley discovers that the Taloulians make little distinction between their daily round of activities and their modes of worship and celebration. Indeed it appears that life for his hosts is a species of continual performance. This is eminent grist to his mill for he begins to fantasise ways in which *The Mikado*'s happy ending might also consist in the happy resolution of his own and fellow captives' fate. This discovery results from the trying-on of a wig destined to render the actor understudying the Mikado completely bald, thus enabling him to wear a tight fitting cap whose snake-like protuberance arises from the crown on internal scaffolding and bounces to left and right with menacing unpredictability. Far from impressed by this millinery confection, the Taloulians, whose own head-dresses are invariably creative, become most agitated at the sight. It transpires that the egg-shaped head of the actor in question has innocently signified the celestial placenta and inadvertently transformed him into a map of the Taloulian cosmos. Further conversation – thanks to the obliging Portuguese trader – reveals that the entire village actually functions as a representation of divine spatial order from the disposition of King Talou's palace to the layout and cultivation of fields, weaving designs and where the men and women sleep. Stanley's eyes glisten at the sophistication of his hosts' perception of the world; gradually, the lineaments of his musical diversion begin – like jungle creepers and unknown varieties of ivy – to proliferate and strengthen in his mind and *The Mikado* commences its transmigration into a type of Grand Opera, perhaps of a sort to which Mr Sullivan himself has so often aspired but with so little result.

Thus it is revealed that the very bodies of the three little maids from school are in fact singing mnemonic maps for, as Kalulu and his friends don their kimonos, the migration path of their mythical ancestral heroes is shown to be inscribed upon the skin of the young men's backs. This tegumentary inscription or 'scarification' as Stanley calls it, depicts the horizon line or 'back' of Lake Tanganyika while simultaneously signifying the Milky Way and Orion's Belt in the night sky. Suddenly, Stanley perceives that Gilbert's line from the Maids' song, 'Freed from its genius tutelary' whose touching comic punch derives much of its humour from syntactic inversion and strained rhyme, might, by virtue of the metaphysical wires crossed in these changed circumstances, drink deeply of the spirits of this place and affect its listeners as immortal poetry.

*

the tiny inflorescence of the fig took merry down merry down pollen on its tongue and the song filled up its glades with hornbills mousebirds and all the things of shreds and patches

*

In so hot a climate water is central to life and Stanley has not been surprised to discover that the care and respect due to its gods is impressed upon the young Taloulians from an early age. The magical dimensions of the village make this duty much easier and Stanley realises that he must take it, in its entirety, as his stage. Scenes and acts will be replaced by processions of singers moving from one pregnant site to another. In particular, the Grand Finale, focused on the Mikado's forgiveness, would be choreographed to the map of mythic waters drawn weekly by the village children in their lessons about the different types of water and their linkages with each other. These outdoor water maps drawn upon the ground feature the ancestor Tarourou learning of its properties and creative powers.

To be brief: this performance of *The Mikado* is a notable success and is reckoned by guests and hosts alike to be among the most moving spectacles they have ever participated in or witnessed. So much so, however, that the Mikado, King Talou himself that is, succumbs to an irresistible desire to tour the show the length and breadth of his kingdom. As his kingdom is twice the size of Wales this is no mean undertaking. Far from being dismayed by this prospect, though, Stanley seems curiously resigned and rationalises his ravishment at the brown hands of the young water gods by intimating to his party that they might make good their escape during the relative chaos their operatic tour will entail.

*

Know then that the strong musky odour of the Baobab Tree attracts the gentlemen of Japan who build their colonial nests in luminous white blossoms the size of saucers and tap into the water table with their nancies on their knees

*

About a year into this outreach mission, *The Mikado* comes to the southern borders of the kingdom. No escape has been effected and the name of the good Dr Livingstone has not passed Stanley's lips in several months. Obsessed by the details of each performance and entranced by the need to alter each one to the specific spiritual contours of individual villages, Stanley now travels in a strange hybrid country, his mind full of the sound of kimonos rustling through savannah grassland and the slippery English vowels of Kalulu's little maid.

By the month of June they reach the village of Ujiji. At around six in the evening the performance has reached its final act. As ever, the tutelary waters of the place dictate the stage directions: Poo Bah, Ko-Ko, Katisha and Pitti Sing are grouped around the 'water that feeds the wells' petitioning the Mikado – who stands appropriately at 'water of the master' – for mercy. A little to one side Kalulu, alias Yum Yum, stares devotedly across 'water of the womb' at Stanley, aka Nankee Pooh, who kneels in a space named 'secret water'. In this particular village, which relies upon mnemonic devices made out of beads and other objects, the usual pagoda has been converted to the shape of a large cowrie shell that forms a suitable backdrop to the action.

75

Yum Yum and Nankee have reached their final ecstatic duet and are singing their cotton socks off:

> The threatened cloud has passed away
> And brightly shines the dawning day;
> What though the night may come too soon,
> We've years and years of afternoon.

when a sudden commotion disrupts the crowd of watching spectators and a most curious sight stops all the singers in their tracks. Two short but sturdy native men walk forward carrying what seems to be a log that they place reverently on the ground in the middle of the performance space. 'What is the meaning of this impertinence?' cries Stanley, quite outraged at an interruption so close to his final consummation with Yum Yum.

The Portuguese trader, who has accompanied them uncomplainingly on all their journeys and become an invaluable prompt, intervenes and is soon able to convey to Stanley the momentous information that the log is no ordinary log but a coffin bearing the mortal remains of Dr David Livingstone.

*

'What I should have said to him had I met him alive!' cries Stanley to the assembled spectators, falling on his knees before the log and touching it as if it were a holy relic. All memory of the performance in which he has just been engaged seems to have vanished. He retains sufficient presence of mind, however, to have the log-coffin transported to an empty granary outwith the village walls and there proceeds to unpack the contents in order to be sure of the deceased's identity. First, a layer of N'gambe bark is stripped away; this in turn reveals a piece of sailcloth within which they uncover a cylinder made from the bark of a Myonga tree and then, finally, doll-like, his knees tucked up beneath his chin, wrapped in the fabric of some calico, the sun-dried, eviscerated body of David Livingstone emerges.

*

This 'coup de théâtre' conveys an appropriate sense of closure but my father's annotations to the libretto I have summarised above clearly states that no conclusive indication is given that the opera definitely ends in this manner. It is, of course, imperative that I should be clear on this point. The curious tale of Stanley's encounter with Livingstone which I have just related forms the climax of a little known, never performed opera entitled *Impressions of Africa* by the Czech composer Victor Ullman and the librettist Petr Kien, who both perished tragically in a German concentration camp. My father, who had been active during the 1950s and 1960s in introducing little known operas to the public via the Glasgow Grand Opera Society, had discovered this piece in the city's Mitchell Library. How it had come to rest so far from its place of creation has never been discovered. A number of inconsistencies, indeed, give rise to worrying concerns as to its genuineness. In a marginal note near the start of the libretto, my father has pencilled two dates. The first one, 1873, is the year of Dr Livingstone's death. 1885 saw the first performance of *The Mikado*. It may be surmised, of course, that Ullman and Kien were in no position to check such details and the engaging spirit of this opera is akin to that of the satirical *The Emperor of Atlantis*, composed before their deportation from the camp at Theresienstadt. It has always been assumed, however, that no other work was written before they were murdered. It is clear from my father's papers that he intended 'The Grand' to produce this opera and that he should play the role of Stanley. It is not clear why he failed in his endeavour.

Tae Rimbaud

eftir thi Arabic of Mou'in Bsissou

When Rimbaud turned tae slavin
an cast his net ower Abyssinia
doolandered the black lion an meltit
the pelican he gave po eh ry the Vicky
och he wiz awfie loyal so he wiz oor kid
but there's a gey muckle lot at wur po ehs
an turned tae slavin,
tae pochlin,
wi oot geein po eh ry the Vicky
they became gallus ad agency reps
dealers in fake paintins
wi oot geein po eh ry the Vicky at aw at aw
in ra bosses palaces, their wee pomes became
doors an windies,
tables an rugs
but they didny gie po eh ry the Vicky och no
they done the 'Come away Scoatlan!' til they wur boky-fu
got wally dugs an titles aff aw the warl's high-heid-yins,
the gold, the siller an the keechy medal
but did they gie po eh ry the V? Naw, naw.
no ataw.
the polis' pawprint
the manky soles o yon polismen jungle-jim their pomes
but och no, no ataw, they huvny ivver, nivver ivver
gien po eh ry the Vicky.
Right noble that Rimbaud,
right leal belter
ole bampot Rimbaud.

Doolander – give a heavy blow; melt – bash; Vicky – a Glaswegian term for a rude
V–sign; pochle – steal; boky-fu – drunk, overstuffed with comestibles to the point of
wishing to vomit; wally dugs – dogs made of porcelain; high-heid-yin – boss; keechy
– shitty; leal – loyal; belter – something or someone excellent; bampot – a nutcase.

A Walk

Literature falls away
and every reference to a world
beyond this series of linked ponds.

There is
every kind of bird
– for once I will not name them –
trees, all types,

perpetual rustlings,
a wind that is barely human
and I take my dead father
by the hand and walk

with him: three times
we walk around this water,
skirting, just skirting
and then I let him go

but this moment
which is far the hardest pain
remains

'Knock thi'

eftir thi German o Paul Celan

Knock thi
lichtcogs awaw:

thi floatin wurd
is thi darkenin's

Darkenin – twilight, dusk.

Baines His Dissection

Baines His Dissection

i.m. Sir John Finch (1626–1682) and Sir Thomas Baines (1622–1680)

for Donny O'Rourke

1 A Procession

For hours now: a little scraping tear,
scratchings, a dab, a blot; then it runs
again – blue, red – coagulates tired
eyes, swims in tears: the quill tears up
the grain of paper, reflecting it away
like skin, finger-forceps grip tense
the flap, scalp through deep fascia
to the muscles of sense.
That scrape again. Is it me
or the witter of the small barboni fish
hung from cabin beams whose thin blue light
dries out like rotten wood?
The parchment heaves up
with its choppy words, once sheathed
in the fibrous tunic of a Medway oak,
white, fusiform, cleaned, defined,
dissected into compass timber or stretched
tight for sea or study scroll. Beneath bark
this paper vessel ran like ink or blood,
its sap beating in tendons for the coffin
of my friend, Sir Thomas Baines, embalmed in brandy.
He floats next door. Not door. No. Mere canvas,
an indoor sail, still unless moved
by my erratic breath. His trestle glimmers,
looms in the palimpsest of candle-light,
trembles in the harbour's toy troughs and crests.
He spurned play but it got him at the last:
the Ambassador's companion borne in pomp
by twenty-six bostancis, muftis, imams, kadis,
down from Pera, Galatea, wreathed in salutes
of gun-smoke. A cenotaph stood for three days
in the Captain's cabin, covered with a pall,
a sabred dervish by his scutcheon (sable

two bones crosswise argent), six great tapers
burning by in six great silver candlesticks.
'*Monsu arrivar!*' The pidgin Italian of the Turks!
That off-hand, intimate, distant, haughty race,
cruel and playful, obsessed with ceremony,
stopping trade to make fine shows of it
while eleven thousand boys had their prepuces
cut off at the Crown Prince's circumcision.
We witnessed that procession: wagon
upon wagon each with its nesting guild,
shoemakers, tailors, weavers, all set out
with tokens of their art, bakers kneading loaves
the size of hammam domes, smiths stoking
little forges and walking gardens full of flowers
with waxwork fruits held in slings by slaves.
As they kicked up a perfect Egyptian mist of dust
you stood beside me, Tom, and called it
'hobbyhorsism folly!' Silenced by the fireworks battle
though, the Seraglio lit up in a thousand
camphor balls of pure white fire.
Fire, procession, ceremony.
There's something to be said for it
and I'm determined we'll have our own display,
dear Tom, our profession of unusual friendship,
our trade as doctors, diplomats, decked out
upon a Cambridge tomb, our ensigns of affection
flagged up and out for prayerful and tourist to decipher.
Embalmed within that stone or living our spiritual life
like the ghosts of holy Turks beside their kiosks,
we'll move as we have always done in one harmonious
cavalcade, two bodies, one soul, the craft of love.
Except there is for now one person less
and I, John Finch, Ambassador to the Porte,
am less in consequence; 'Dosti!', 'Dear Friend!'
'Aman!' 'Janum!' 'Mercy!' 'My Soul!' 'Kuzum!'
'My Lamb!', unsteadily I grip your coffin's berth
and look through a glass to your face below,
spirits of wine preserve its peaceful countenance
and momentarily it swells beneath my gaze
as if caught up in drops of oil spat out
by divers to magnify the minute objects of the deep.
My spirit diver, swim beside me on our voyage
home, protect me from storm and mermaid
and the ebb and flow of memory.

2 An Anatomy

We are goat born, my Baines,
like Marsyas, fit only to be flayed,
little worlds of inner secrets
split by the lynx-like knife.
In Padua and Pisa I got those skills
which I can turn on you in intimacies
of autopsy without a flinch: my love,
my work now perfectly combined.
Our Muslim surgeons could not oblige
and so I incise and cut, scour
brain and abdomen, aspirate gases
with a trocar. Where the heart beat
I place musk, sweet-basil in the kidney-bed,
quince in ala of the sacrum.
Saffron, violets, ambergris attack bacteria.
I repack the skull with honey.
Spooning in Constantinople moonlight
just a month before the end
I noticed how your nape grew dark hairs yet,
recalled how thirty-six years ago, snug
in the same view, I imagined how each one
would be white one day. It gave me hope.
'*Una mana con occhio!*' 'A hand with eyes!'
whose skill could kindle infinite desire
now excavates the bladder for stones
that led you to your tomb. Irony
and renal colic were the dead ends
of distorted crypts that burrowed out
the ureteric musculature.
How you strained to void those philosophic calculi,
another joke that made you smile through pain.
And yet those phosphate stones
had serious facets too: 'Lapis est,
quem Salomonis architecti rejecerunt.'
What niche for us in the Temple
of King Solomon's England?
And so we rolled in exile across Europe,
gathering the moss of learning, liberty, love.
Royal servants, yes, but at a distance.
I stone the body of my lover, eviscerate
and then the glorious mineral

in three days reconstitutes itself.
As cousin Harvey's good friend Donne once wrote:
'He was all gold when he lay
down but rose all tincture!'
Oh, Tom! The alchemists have myriad names for you:
body of magnesia, the light of lights,
marvellous father, fugitive servant.
You are rubine stone and chaos,
toad, green lion, virgin's milk.
You are Brazil! Or simply 'Fava'
as our Italians called you, hearing 'bean' for Baines!
No matter! But that's not *quite* the point:
matter *and* spirit, spirit *in* matter
to conjure until it effervesces
like the semen which seems contagious
for Harvey found no trace of it
within the ovum after sex.
How else explain the love of like for like
as well as different? Our Cambridge tutors
had the gist of it before modern science
got there too. They flew above the high and airy
hills of Platonism, disdained democritism
which so embases and enthralls.
More and Cudworth, good men who studied
to spiritualise their bodies not to incarnate
their souls, who thought Heaven first a temper,
then a place. In his enthusiastic middle age,
More shook like a Quaker in the threshold
of his body, tasting distinctions
in the cabalistic weather as our ship's captain
tries the *imbat* which will carry us to sea.
That warm wind proves, to paraphrase Ficino,
that spirit is a very subtle body, almost soul,
not a soul and almost body. So, bent upon
this clotted and compacted corpse
I pare away the veins, capillaries and arteries,
reveal that luciform and attenuate vehicle,
transparent stone stuck in my balm of unguents.
Poor Baines, caught in a coat of resin
and pinned within a tree!
We are like tortoises in the Age of Tulips:
we strap small lamps upon our backs
and creep among the parterres of the night

so the distant think we are light itself
or tulips strolling among tulips.
Suspended disbelief! The tortoises
circle lamplight endlessly among the Gardens
of Felicity, small ventricles of light slowly
pulsing through the tulip fields as blood
pumps out to the periphery and then returns,
preserved. Yet cousin Harvey acknowledged
with *Leviticus* that the blood *is* soul,
numinous *and* turgescent, matter *and* force
as long as it moves in vessels: *cor a currendo*,
not this sorry *cruor*, this gore
I mop from the dissection table.
And so we moved continuously, sharing *mot*
et motion. When coaches failed we hired sedans
and grew a self so interpersonal each could say
'I think, therefore, we are.' Wherever
the Red Apple of dominion settled
we were Zeno's arrow, shaft and quiver,
barely different, presenting motion
and then decamping. Out. Elsewhere.

3 Dallam's Fantasy

I return to Cambridge on the *Oxford*.
Spires shuffle in my memory, changeable
as the very spindle of the main top mast
or wamblings of my stomach which shears
off according to the motions of the *Euripus*.
I sip a little sack and wormwood to calm
the humours, but England, the world even,
a poet may someday say is as variable
as the *Euripus*. It waxes, wanes with ages
of the moon. When we first loved each other
it seemed to be an isle of bells, debate
and woodsmoke wafting over playing fields,
annealed to the Universe by amber cupolas.
A steady place. And so it was. But steadiness
runs deep and from the depths our masters
looked at us and seeing chaos
where only difference lurked or a surfeit of similitude

suggested silence or torture for sedition.
We linked hands and left. First Paris
where I rejoiced to see old Calvin's house
reduced to a dunghill, fit epitaph
for the man who burnt Servetus on a pyre
for proposing the lesser circulation
of the blood. And then our tour of Italy
which lasted twenty-two good years:
we made Pro-Rector, Syndic of Padua University,
Resident at Florence to the Grand Duke of Tuscany;
Ambassador, we learned to deal in trade capitulations
while great physicians of the day,
Malphighi, Borelli, Fracassati, Truttwyn
called us friends. When we went home
it was to be knighted, doctors to the Queen.
But in between it was as if our country also left:
one king lost his head, a farmer ruled,
around 1650 some folk noticed, really noticed
America was there and that the moon
and other planets perhaps existed for themselves
and not for us. New ways of praying
flak the air like volleys of small shot
and in the dim, dank lanes of London wynds
they open places for 'our kind'. 'Our kind'!
The fact that I can say this is the point.
And others say it too and persecute *and* tolerate.
We did not like this either and so we left again.
Plurality does not concern the Turks.
Severe but subtle they denote rank by perfume,
are not afraid if the religions of their Empire mingle too.
Nationality is a career 'and not a cause'.
Beauty not gender is seductive.
When passion left us, I was lonely
and now I face the final loneliness.
But then we discovered, together and separately,
the bow-like eyebrows of tall Persians,
how good Armenians or silver-chested Greeks
feel against the cold, that Baghdad boys
like torturing 'and never keep appointments'.*
So the flavour of our happiness had gradations
that would surprise a superintendent of fine sherbets.
Not *being* but *coming* into being was our forte.
Seamen, semen, pneumatic blood concurred.

Even plague whose venomous and sticky atoms
took up abode in miasmatic air and chased us
from the city to a town of tents and back again.
And yet, and *so* I cannot stay. For even
'the Refuge of the World' has blind spots.
I cannot live well in a city crawling with calligraphy,
weltering in words that banish even as they gesture
in and to the stones they're written on. Nothing
can be left to contemplation, the partially
uninstructed stare. No pictures here then,
no simulacra of the human, little music
which is a spirit like our own. How the ship's bells
peel me back to Cambridge from the drone of muezzin!
Another shape wavers through the canvas
by my Baines' coffin, it too a wrack of organs:
Dallam's mechanical fantasy,
a gift from old Queen Bess to some forgotten Sultan,
is now sent back 'to be repaired', in fact
is banished for its display of personages
which stand at two corners of the second story,
lift trumpets to their heads and sound a tantarra.
In better times this organ played a song of five parts
twice over and on the casement top did sit
a holly bush full of blackbirds and thrushes
which at the music's end sang and shook their wings.
Why did it offend so much? When Baines
had audience with the Vani Effendi he was told
the Blessed went not into Paradise
until the Day of Judgement but had continual
sight of it through one great window.
Perhaps he sees it from his little porthole now.
Is the principle not the same? We veer
predictably, our tack on the divine
is rude and artificial. We stand on tip-toe
at a threshold or a casement and then are flung
upon the cabin floor made giddy by our reach
and lack of it. But after the Marmarean sunset,
the gentle jangling of that instrument,
as the ship slides over into sleep,
stirs my blood like tulip-wine and I hear my lover
slip his veins of oak and colonise the organ
moving it ineffably. Then he sees and seizes me
in sound, his eyes, two knarled cherry plugs

of song, rush forth on tiny thrushes wings
like butterfies of soul. His hair enwreathes
the cabin with arias that wake the sap
in coffined wood and crescendo on a note
so pure it dissects me as I shiver
in my hammock's pitch. The air becomes
a partial gauze: minims, quavers, blackbirds
stick to its interstices, waft a web
of tenor chirrups which then break off,
float down, a snow of feathered trills
that deliquesce upon my skin, vibrate
the tissues until all the vessels
of this little world are cloaked and magnified
in tune, a music that is his, is mine, is Dallam's
and all the spirits that transport us.

Note

Among the many texts on which I have drawn for this poem I wish to acknowledge particularly the work of Philip Mansel, whose wonderful book *Constantinople: City of the World's Desire, 1453–1924* (Penguin, 1997) was a source of much inspiration. This description of the Armenians, Greeks and Baghdad boys is indebted to his transcription of details taken from Fazil Bey's (1759–1810) *Khubanname* (*The Book of Beauties*). Bey's dates are of course later than those of Finch and Baines, but I hope the reader may allow me this licence on the grounds that the same pleasures were possibly available during the earlier period.

The 'Red Apple' (p. 87) was a Turkish phrase for whichever city was considered to form the capital of the known world.